Maps to Bike Gettys
Battle Days 2 and 3 St
miles) is an educational mini-book
that complements Civil War Cycling's
286-page comprehensive guidebook
for a 23.8-mile tour:

civilwarcycling.com

Bicycling Gettysburg National Military Park:
The Cyclist's Civil War Travel Guide
ISBN 978-1-7326038-0-6 (March 2019)

"Whether you're a cycling enthusiast, history buff, or both, Sue Thibodeau's *Bicycling Gettysburg National Military Park: The Cyclist's Civil War Travel Guide* is a must-have for your next visit to Gettysburg. In fact, this 286-page book is so chock-full of useful maps, photographs, and reference information about the battlefield's monuments, farm buildings, and areas of interest that it should be in the daypack of anybody touring the park and/or town of Gettysburg."

~ *Civil War Times*

"*Bicycling Gettysburg* is comprehensible to readers and riders of all ages and expertise... concise and readable for both aficionados and novices."

~ *Civil War Monitor*

"The best ways to truly see a battlefield are by walking and biking. And biking a battlefield such as Gettysburg provides a rush like no other. Sue has produced a valuable book about how to ride that most hallowed Civil War ground. A definite keeper."

~ John Banks, journalist, blogger, author

Maps to Bike Gettysburg

No. 3b

Battle Days 2 & 3 Short Loop

10.7 miles

Sue Thibodeau

A Companion Mini-Book for
Bicycling Gettysburg National Military Park

Maps to Bike Gettysburg No. 3b:
Battle Days 2 & 3 Short Loop (10.7 miles)

Copyright © 2021 Sue Thibodeau

Map Rendering Copyright © 2019 Sue Thibodeau
Map Data Copyright © OpenStreetMap contributors
www.openstreetmap.org/copyright
Liberation Sans Font Family, SIL Open Font License 1.1

Published by Civil War Cycling
154 Cobblestone Court Drive #110, Victor, NY 14564
Digital (PDF) maps sold separately at civilwarcycling.com

ISBN 978-1-7326038-8-2 (pbk)

20210325-L5-1.5
First Printing

About the Author

Sue Thibodeau is a bicycling enthusiast, computer scientist, and former teacher. "Like a kid on a bike," she explores U.S. national military parks as a way to learn Civil War history. A graduate of Duke University, the University of Notre Dame, and the Rochester Institute of Technology, Sue publishes educational touring materials through Civil War Cycling.

She is the author of *Bicycling Gettysburg National Military Park* (2019); *Bicycling Antietam National Battlefield* (2020); and two forthcoming guidebooks, *Bicycling Chickamauga Battlefield* (2021) and *Bicycling Shiloh National Military Park* (2022).

About this Book

Maps to Bike Gettysburg No. 3b: Battle Days 2 & 3 Short Loop provides color maps and turn-by-turn directions for a safe and educational, 10.7-mile park ride to visit the most famous landmarks of the July 2-3, 1863 battlefield, including Culp's Hill. Designed for a lightweight ride, this book complements Civil War Cycling's more detailed and comprehensive guidebook, *Bicycling Gettysburg National Military Park.*

Maps to Bike Gettysburg No. 3b contains 17 detailed color maps with corresponding bicycle cue tables; 53 color photos; monument GPS points; and micro-histories for learning about the Battle of Gettysburg. It does not duplicate the guidebook's chapters on tour planning ideas; orienteering techniques; battle statistics; historical summaries; or monument descriptions for Route 1's 23.8-mile ride. This mini-book is an expanded print version of the Route 3b digital PDF map that is available at www.civilwarcycling.com/shop/.

Route 3b is a popular route that covers Spangler's Spring, Culp's Hill, East Cemetery Hill, part of Seminary Ridge, The Wheatfield, Devil's Den, Little Round Top, and Cemetery Ridge. Because it cuts east through The Peach Orchard, Route 3b does not cover Warfield Ridge or South Cavalry Field. You will enjoy a a few steep hills—for a cumulative gain of 653'. Plan for a 3–4 hour tour with frequent stops to appreciate the beautiful landscape and some of the park's 1,300+ monuments. Route 3b limits exposure to busy roads; provides route-specific health and safety tips; identifies one-way roads; and notes the location of bicycle racks, water sources, restrooms, and picnic areas.

CONTENTS

A Note About Segment Names: Civil War Cycling creates routes from a set of pre-defined "segments" that have mostly arbitrary alphabetic abbreviations. (This is how we can offer fourteen different routes through Gettysburg). For example, whereas Route 1 consists of a predictable name sequence, Segments A–L, Route 3b segment names are less predictable.

The naming convention is unimportant to your ride; simply follow Route 3b in the order presented in this book.

Preface

For more than thirty years, and over many dozens of visits, I toured Gettysburg National Military Park by bus, car, and foot. In 2012, I toured the battlefield on a bicycle for the first time. The experience of learning American history while exploring park land on a bicycle is hard to describe, but if I had to pick one word, it would be "exhilarating." And yet it took four years to work out the kinks in my self-directed, solo tours. I was frustrated by one-way roads, incomplete or inaccurate maps, and not knowing how best to avoid town traffic. But I looked forward to every trip, and enjoyed them all.

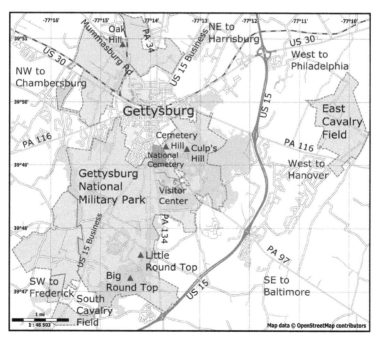

Map P.1. Gettysburg, Pennsylvania

Eventually, I learned what equipment to pack, what clothes to wear, and where to find convenient access to water, portable toilets, and shade for picnics. It was also challenging to know how best to sequence my visitation of monuments and within what general timeframe. I created my own maps (and guidebook) because I could not find any maps that met the needs of a bicycling historian. I hope that these maps help you to avoid the mistakes that I had made and that you can enjoy every minute of your battlefield tour.

In September 2018, I designed twelve digital PDF document maps that collectively define fourteen bicycle loops through the Gettysburg battlefield. The maps are available for secure online purchase and download from the Civil War Cycling website. Note: These digital files are not part of a GPS navigation system, and you will need Adobe's free PDF reader to view or print the maps and directions for your Gettysburg cycling tour.

Route #	Route Name	Miles
1	Full Day Loop	23.8
1b	Full Day Short Loop	11.5
2	Battle Day 1 Loop	10.5
3	Battle Days 2 & 3 Loop	17.0
3b	**Battle Days 2 & 3 Short Loop**	**10.7**
4	The Ridges Loop	9.0
5	The Ridges Extended Loop	12.2
6,7	Culp's Hill Lower & Upper Loops	2.4 (ea)
8	Culp's Hill Double Loop	5.5
9–11	Devil's Den, The Wheatfield, and Little Round Top Loops	1.5–3.8
12	East Cavalry Field	5.2

Table of Gettysburg Bicycle Routes

For descriptions and details, visit Civil War Cycling at www.civilwarcycling.com/battlefields/gettysburg/routes/.

Given the popularity of the digital maps—and their appeal to bicyclists who want specifically themed historical rides over varying distances—I launched a paperback mini-book series in 2021 called *Maps to Bike Gettysburg*. Each mini-book is part of an independently usable set of educational publications. They are an expanded subset of Civil War Cycling's comprehensive guidebook for a 23.8-mile tour, *Bicycling Gettysburg National Military Park* (2019).

Maps to Bike Gettysburg No. 3b is one book in a short series of highly focused and portable travel guides. It provides maps, GPS points, monument photos, and micro-histories for Route 3b, "Battle Days 2 & 3 Short Loop," a 10.7-mile ride through the Gettysburg battlefield park. As its name suggests, it provides an abbreviated tour of the southern half of the Gettysburg battlefield so that you can enjoy the spectacular ride up to (and down!) Culp's Hill.

My hope is that the *Maps to Bike Gettysburg* mini-book series will appeal to bicyclists who want short but detailed printed maps and bicycling directions for a variety of routes. Most bicyclists who enjoy learning history on two wheels will want to return to Gettysburg for many more rides. "Maps to Bike Gettysburg" gives you that option.

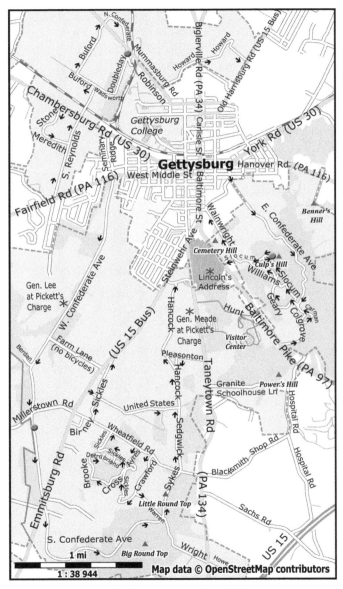

Map P.2. Gettysburg Park Roads

1.   Getting Your Mind In Gear

Many people feel a strong desire to visit and then return again to Gettysburg. We struggle to explain our connection to the land and the people who lived and died here. While exploring the battlefield park on two wheels, bicyclists know well the extraordinary feeling that Joshua Chamberlain described in 1889:

> *In great deeds something abides. On great fields something stays. Forms change and pass; bodies disappear, but spirits linger, to consecrate ground for the vision-place of souls. And reverent men and women from afar, and generations that know us not and that we know not of, heart-drawn to see where and by whom great things were suffered and done for them, shall come to this deathless field to ponder and dream...* ~Col. Joshua Lawrence Chamberlain, "Dedication of the 20th Maine Monuments," October 3, 1889, Gettysburg.

This book will take you on a bicycle tour that allows the monuments and the Gettysburg landscape to teach you Civil War history. As a mini-book, it is deliberately brief and yet packed with color maps and turn-by-turn directions for a 10.7-mile bike ride. For a full educational experience, the reader is encouraged to consult Civil War Cycling's comprehensive guidebook, *Bicycling Gettysburg National Military Park.*

The Battle of Gettysburg (1863)

In 1863, Gen. Robert E. Lee and his Confederate Army of Northern Virginia invaded Pennsylvania through Maryland and bore down on Gettysburg from the north. To meet the threat, the newly promoted Maj.

Gen. George G. Meade rallied the Union Army of the Potomac and advanced toward Gettysburg from the south. About 170,000 soldiers converged on this farming town, home to roughly 2,400 citizens, ten miles north of the Maryland border. After three days of fighting on July 1–3, Lee's army was defeated but allowed to retreat back to Virginia. It was the deadliest battle in U.S. military history:

	Union	Confederate	Total
Dead:	3,155	3,903	7,058
Wounded:	14,529	18,735	33,264
Missing/Captured:	5,365	5,425	10,790
Total:	23,049	28,063	51,112

Table 1.1. Gettysburg Casualties

Source: American Battlefield Trust, battlefields.org/learn/civil-war/battles/gettysburg.

A Visual Summary of the Battle—Five Maps

The next five pages summarize the Battle of Gettysburg as a sequence of five military maps. These maps are *deliberately impressionistic* and designed for the overall purpose of learning on-the-go. (Please consult a military atlas if you require more detail).

Army-level battle lines have a blurred look to suggest approximate positions that a bicyclist can commit to memory without having to juggle the names of corps, divisions, or regiments. Union lines are blue and Confederate lines are red. Military positions overlay a modern road network so that bicyclists can easily orient themselves on the battlefield and also understand the high-level battle narrative in the context of one's current location.

July 1, 1863—Wednesday

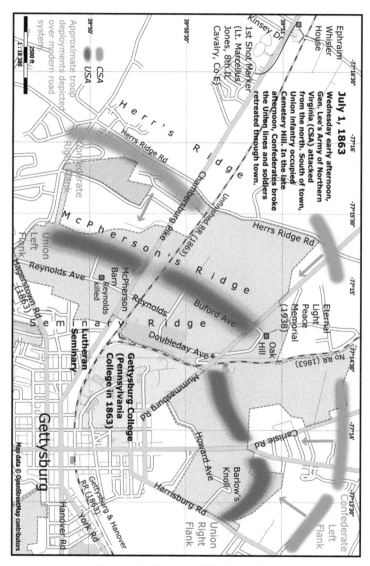

July 1, 1863
Wednesday early afternoon, Gen. Lee's Army of Northern Virginia (CSA) attacked from the north. South of town, Union infantry occupied Cemetery Hill. In the late afternoon, Confederates broke the Union lines and soldiers retreated through town.

Ephraim Whisler House

Kinsey Dr

1st Shot Marker (Lt. Marcellus Jones, 8th IL Cavalry, Co E)

CSA
USA

Approximate troop deployments depicted over modern road system.

2500 ft.
1:18,380

Herr's Ridge

Herrs Ridge Rd

McPherson's Ridge

Union unfinished RR (1863)

Chambersburg Pike

Confederate Right Flank

Union Left Flank

Reynolds Ave

Hagerstown Rd (1863)

McPherson Barn

Reynolds killed

Reynolds Ave

Seminary Ridge

Lutheran Seminary

Gettysburg College (Pennsylvania College in 1863)

Buford Ave

Doubleday Ave

Mummasburg Rd

Herrs Ridge Rd

Eternal Light Peace Memorial (1938)

Oak Hill

No RR (1863)

Gettysburg

Map data © OpenStreetMap contributors

Howard Ave

Barlow's Knoll

Carlisle Rd

Gettysburg & Hanover RR (1863)

Harrisburg Rd

York Rd

Hanover Rd

Union Right Flank

Confederate Left Flank

Map 1.1. July 1—Wednesday

July 2, 1863—Thursday

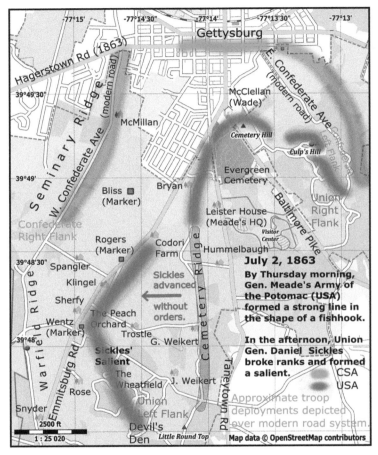

Map 1.2. July 2—Thursday Morning

While riding your bicycle through the Gettysburg battlefield, look for tall natural and physical structures (like Little Round Top or the Pennsylvania and Virginia State Monuments) to help you to stay oriented using this book's maps.

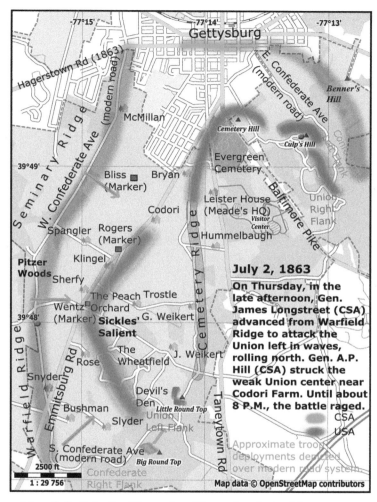

Map 1.3. July 2—Thursday Thursday Late Afternoon

Gettysburg barns have a distinctive shape, especially the three-steeple Codori barn. If you take the time to place them on a map, the battlefield story is easier to understand.

July 2 & 3, 1863—Battle for Culp's Hill

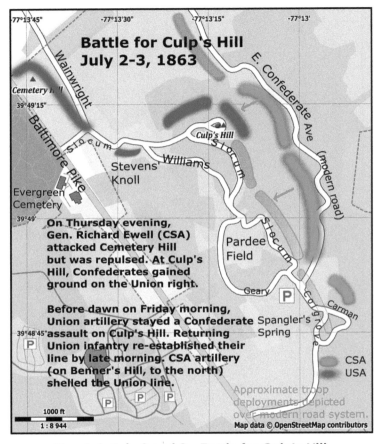

Map 1.4. July 2 and 3—Battle for Culp's Hill

Touring busses are not permitted in the Culp's Hill area, and so, Culp's Hill is not part of the official NPS auto tour. For bicyclists, this much neglected battlefield site offers a beautiful but relatively steep, tree-lined ride. Civil War Cycling's Route 3b mini-book will take you on a bike tour of Spangler's Spring and Culp's Hill.

July 3, 1863—Pickett's Charge

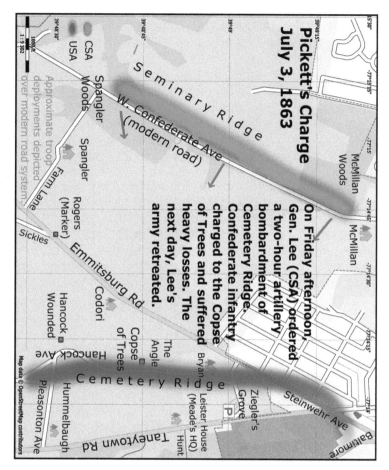

Map 1.5. July 3—Pickett's Charge

A walk in the fields of Pickett's Charge—which is a one-mile hike from Seminary to Cemetery Ridge—will broaden your understanding of the impact of geography on the results of the battle. The attack is named for Confederate Maj. Gen. George E. Pickett.

Gettysburg National Military Park

After the U.S. Civil War, former Union Maj. Gen. Daniel E. Sickles sponsored legislation to establish a national military park in Gettysburg, Pennsylvania. He introduced H.R. 8096 in 1894, and Congress approved the bill in 1895. Since that time, Gettysburg National Military Park has grown to more than 6,000 acres under the management of the National Park Service. For modern maps of park roads and geography, see Map P.2 on p. 12 and Map 1.6 on p. 21, respectively.

Today, most roads in Gettysburg National Military Park are named after Union officers of the Army of the Potomac. The shape of each park road roughly matches the battlefield formation for the soldiers under that officer's command. This park feature can be very helpful to bicyclists who want to understand the battlefield story relative to one's current location. For example, the broken and angled shape of Sickles Avenue depicts Sickles' tenuous 3rd Corps line on July 2, 1863. You can see this by matching Sickles' line shown on Map 1.3 with Sickles Avenue on Map P.2.

At Gettysburg, the NPS maintains more than 1,300 monuments and markers. There are eighteen state monuments on Seminary and Cemetery Ridges. Throughout the park stand eight large equestrian monuments (six Union and two Confederate generals) and many more bronze portrait statues. Most of Gettysburg's monuments are dedicated to regiments in the Army of the Potomac, although you will find many Confederate markers and cast-iron tablets.

Clearly, it is well beyond the scope of this mini-book to identify more than a small sampling of monuments that you will find while riding Route 3b.

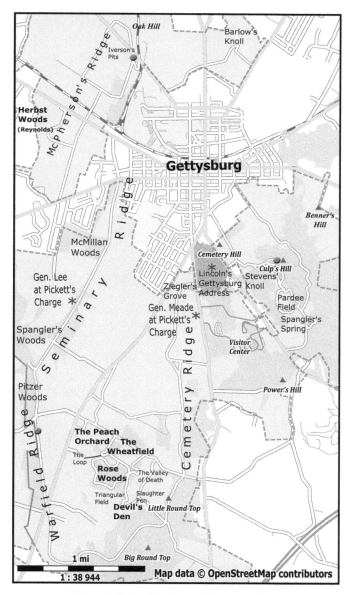

Map 1.6. Gettysburg Geography

Maps to Bike Gettysburg No. 3b

Battle Days 2 & 3 Short Loop (No. 3b)

Route 3b, the "Battle Days 2 & 3 Short Loop," is a 10.7-mile scenic ride up to Culp's Hill followed by a tour of Seminary Ridge and Cemetery Ridge. It covers the main Confederate and Union battle lines for July 2 and 3, 1863. See Map 1.7, p.24.

Most Civil War Cycling routes begin and end at 945 Baltimore Pike, currently near a hotel and 0.5 miles north of the Gettysburg National Military Park (GNMP) Visitor Center. This location simplifies the design of safe, convenient, and circular routes that are composed of reusable segments (more on that, below). It is also close to the GNMP Bus/RV parking, where there are restrooms and water, and to the Spangler's Spring Parking Lot (another possible starting point).

We begin Route 3b by riding south on Baltimore Pike to enter the Culp's Hill area on the east side of the pike. Although Baltimore Pike is a major road, its shoulders are wide on both sides. After passing through Spangler's Spring and riding up Culp's Hill, we tour East Cemetery Hill and then zigzag through residential streets to head south on Seminary Ridge. At Millerstown Road, we cut east to tour The Wheatfield, Devil's Den, and Little Round Top before riding north on Cemetery Ridge and back to our starting point. See Map 1.6 on p. 21, and Map 1.7 on p. 24.

Understanding Segment Maps

Route 3b is one of fourteen Gettysburg bicycling routes published by Civil War Cycling. Each route is designed by chaining together a series of "segments" that function as "building blocks" for creating routes. Although Route 1 consists of Segments A through L, in

Introduction

order, other routes contain a different number and ordering of segments. Route 3b consists of nine segments that total 10.7 miles.

The odometer readings in this book are accurate to +/- 0.05 mile but can vary based on your riding style and equipment. Detailed directions in the form of cue tables will help confirm your location on the battlefield.

Table 1.2. Map and Symbol Key

Gettysburg National Military Park

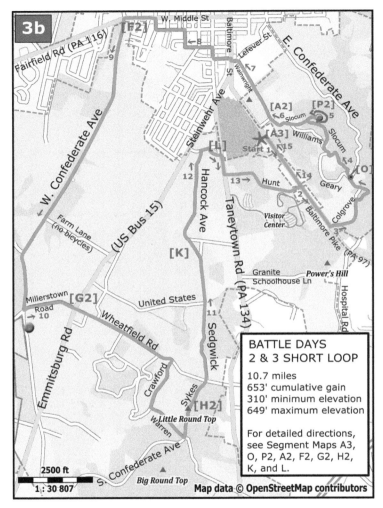

Map 1.7. Route 3b Overview Map

Maps, turn-by-turn directions, and monument highlights for each segment follow. You will start at A3 and ride south to the Culp's Hill Area Entrance. Then ride these segments: O, P2, A2, F2, G2, H2, K, and L.

Understanding Bicycle Cues

Bicycle "cues" are short instructions for completing a route. Each segment map has a corresponding cue table that may use these abbreviations:

◀L	Turn Left	R▶	Turn Right
◀QL	Quick Left	QR▶	Quick Right
◀BL	Bear Left	BR▶	Bear Right
PoL	Pass on Left	PoR	Pass on Right
CS	Continue Straight	ST	Straight Through
SS	Stop Sign	TL	Traffic Light
X	Cross	U	U-Turn
DE	Dead-End	T	T Intersection
UM	Un-Marked	Y	Y Intersection
RR	Railroad	b/c	Becomes
N	North	E	East
S	South	W	West

Table 1.3. Bicycle Cue Abbreviations

Park road signs are often not located or visible at a point at which bicyclists need to make a turning decision. They are black cast iron signs that lie close to the ground. Refer to the maps and cue tables for help. Also, route detours (if any) are highlighted in gray and optionally replace the previous listed instruction.

Finding Battlefield Monuments

Segment maps have white-on-green numbers that identify a small number of featured monuments. For detailed coverage and photos of 100+ monuments, see the guidebook, *Bicycling Gettysburg National Military Park*. You can use both books together but for different purposes. For example, you could read the guidebook before your trip and carry this mini-book on your ride.

Park Bicycling Policies & Town Ordinances

The road network at Gettysburg National Military Park is designed to keep motor vehicles moving in one direction, which means there are many one-way roads. This can be a problem for bicyclists, since not having a pre-planned route can result in feeling frustrated at having to ride many miles to get to a point only a few hundred yards away. Fortunately, if you use Civil War Cycling's maps and directions, you can ride a loop that follows one-way signs. It is worth noting, however, that GNMP policies explicitly allow bicyclists to ride against the flow of traffic within the park (see Section 36, CFR 4.30, *Superintendent's Compendium*, 2016). But not everyone wants to risk confusing motor vehicle drivers.

As for sidewalks in downtown Gettysburg, bicyclists may ride on sidewalks, unless posted otherwise, but they must yield to pedestrians (Code 3-106). Please note that although Gettysburg is a relatively small town, motor vehicle traffic is often congested and bicycle lanes are rare. Even if you are an expert road cyclist, for example, the approach to the Lutheran Seminary while riding on West Middle Street can be dangerous due fast-moving truck traffic on this steep hill with no bicycle lane (but there is a sidewalk). The maps in this book will identify sidewalk options for your consideration.

At the Gettysburg Museum & Visitor Center, "riders should walk their bikes while on pedestrian walks and trails." Not surprisingly, off-road riding is prohibited (www.nps.gov/gett/planyourvisit) in GNMP. You may walk your bicycle at the national cemetery. And finally, check the "Alerts & Conditions" page on the park website before your ride; this site is regularly updated: https://www.nps.gov/gett/planyourvisit/conditions.htm.

2. Let's Go! Bike Route 3b

Route 3b Synopsis

Difficulty	Easy (for most healthy tourists)
Time	3–4 hours (frequent stops)
Distance	10.7 miles
Cumulative Gain	653 feet
Historical Focus	Battle of Gettysburg Days 2 & 3
Geography	Spangler's Spring, Culp's Hill, East Cemetery Hill, northern half of Seminary Ridge, The Wheatfield, Devil's Den, Little Round Top, and Cemetery Ridge
Safety	Mostly 25 mph park roads (1.0 miles on Baltimore Pike; 1.1 miles on residential streets)

Spangler's Spring and Culp's Hill

Unlike Route 5's 12.2-mile tour—which includes full coverage of the Confederate battle lines on Seminary Ridge and South Cavalry Field—Route 3b is a shorter ride through those areas in favor of adding Spangler's Spring and Culp's Hill. For a longer and more complete tour, you may want to consider Route 3. Its 17.0 miles includes the most complete coverage of the Battle of Gettysburg on July 2–3, 1863.

Another option for including Culp's Hill on your tour is to follow Route 3b and then Route 8, the Culp's Hill Double Loop 8 (5.5 miles). These and other Civil War Cycling routes are available as PDF downloads at: civilwarcycling.com/shop/.

Segment A3 (to Spangler's Spring)

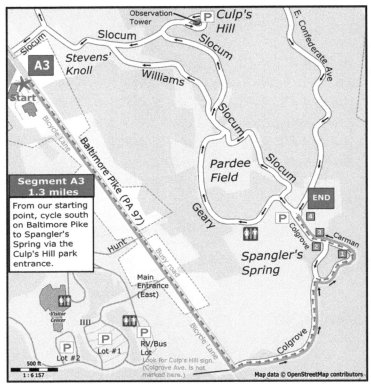

Map 2.1. Route 3b Segment A3 (1.3 miles)

Although Baltimore Pike is a busy public road, your 0.5-mile ride south to the Culp's Hill Area Entrance offers wide shoulders. On the other hand, if you are not staying at the hotel marked by the blue star on the A3 map, you may want to begin at the GNMP RV/Bus Lot for a short 0.1-mile ride on Baltimore Pike; or start at the Spangler's Spring Parking Lot near [2] in the above map. Remember: White-on-green numbers identify monuments whose photos are on the following pages.

Segment A3 Cues (1.3 miles)

From Hotel at 945 Baltimore Pike south to Spangler's Spring Parking Lot:	Seg	Total
0.0 Ride SOUTH to pass Hunt on LEFT	0.4	**0.4**
0.4 STRAIGHT at Hunt for 0.1 miles	0.5	**0.5**
0.5 STRAIGHT through light at GNMP east entrance for 0.3 miles	0.8	**0.8**
0.8 *Careful* LEFT into Culp's Hill Area (unmarked Colgrove) for 0.2 miles	1.0	**1.0**
1.0 RIGHT on Colgrove, which becomes Carman on bend left	1.1	**1.1**
1.1 STRAIGHT on Colgrove into parking lot	1.3	**1.3**

For each route segment, this book provides photos and short descriptions for a sampling of monuments. The numbers on each map match-up to the photos that follow. GPS coordinates (lat, lon) are also listed.

Segment A3 Monument Highlights

1. 39.81307, -77.21472   **2.** 39.81345, -77.21611

1. 13th New Jersey Monument (1887)

Carman Avenue traces the July 3, 1863 battle line of Col. Ezra A. Carman's 13th New Jersey. The regiment supported the 2nd Massachusetts and 27th Indiana when they charged to lower Culp's Hill.

2. 2nd Massachusetts Monument (1879)

This monument is the first at Gettysburg to mark a regiment's battlefield position. Twenty-three-year-old Lt. Col. Charles R. Mudge died in the July 3 charge.

3. 27th Indiana Monument (1885)

Located on Colgrove Avenue, the 27th Indiana Monument lists 111 (out of 339) casualties in Col. Silas Colgrove's ill-fated charge east to lower Culp's Hill.

4. Indiana State Monument (1971)

In the Spangler's Spring and Culp's Hill areas, Indiana soldiers under Col. Silas Colgrove fought Virginians under Brig. Gen. William E. Smith.

3. 39.81356, -77.21594   **4.** 39.81419, -77.21640

In 1895, the U.S. War Department built a stone structure, shown below, around a natural spring likely used by both Union and Confederate soldiers in 1863.

This next photo shows the start of the climb up Slocum Avenue, named for Union Maj. Gen. Henry Slocum, to lower Culp's Hill at [3] on Map 2.2.

Segment O (Culp's Hill Summit)

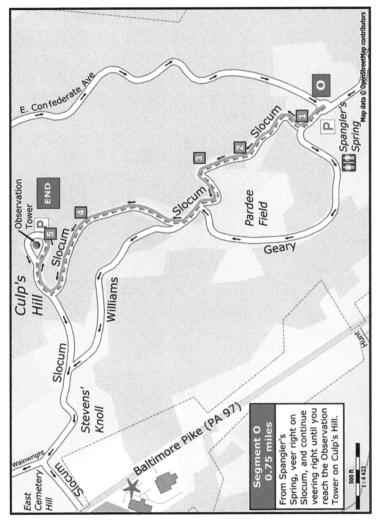

Map 2.2. Route 3b Segment O (0.75 miles)

Tip: At every fork in the road, always veer right.

Segment O Cues (0.75 miles)

For visibility, consider turning on your blinkies.

From Spangler's Spring Parking Lot to Culp's Hill Observation Tower:	Seg	Total
0.0 STRAIGHT through parking lot, RIGHT at fork onto Slocum, uphill to bend. (This is Lower Culp's Hill).	0.2	**1.5**
0.2 Continue downhill, passing Geary on left	0.3	**1.6**
Bear RIGHT at fork to keep on Slocum, passing Williams on left	0.4	**1.7**
0.4 STRAIGHT on Slocum, uphill for 0.3 miles to stop sign	0.7	**2.0**
0.7 RIGHT on Slocum for about 260 feet to Culp's Hill Observation Tower	0.75	**2.05**

Segment O Monument Highlights

1. 39.81479, -77.21689

2. 39.81566, -77.21758

3. 39.81670, -77.21827

4. 39.81924, -77.21973

5. 39.81983, -77.22008

Although Maryland did not secede from the Union, its citizens fought on both sides of the war. At Gettysburg, about one-third of the state's 3,000 soldiers were CSA enlistments.

1. 1st Maryland, Potomac Monument (1888)

This regiment from Frederick, Baltimore, and Washington Counties built breastworks along the slopes of lower Culp's Hill and into this meadow.

2. 3rd Maryland Monument (1888)

Led by a Hungarian wood carver, Col. Joseph M. Sudsburg, the regiment built breastworks in this area.

3. 2nd Maryland (CSA) Monument (1886)

Located at lower Culp's Hill, this monument marks the position of CSA Marylanders on July 2 (evening).

4. 1st Maryland, Eastern Shore Monument (1888)

This untried Union regiment from slaveholding counties in Maryland crushed their Maryland CSA counterparts, but also provided medical aid. The color sergeants for the opposing regiments were cousins.

5. George S. Greene Statue (1907)

Brig. Gen. George Greene's 12th Corps division held Culp's Hill despite being outnumbered while under Confederate infantry attack on July 2–3. Affectionately known as "Pop" Greene, at sixty-two years old, he was the oldest Union general at Gettysburg.

In anticipation of your ride down Culp's Hill in Segment P2 (Map 2.3), the following photo captures the end of a very enjoyable but fast glide down to Stevens' Knoll and the Slocum Equestrian Monument.

Segment P2 (to East Cemetery Hill)

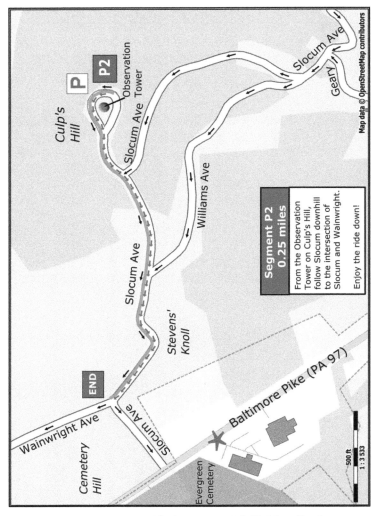

Map 2.3. Route 3b Segment P2 (0.25 miles)

Tip: Watch for car traffic merging from your left.

Segment P2 Cues (0.25 miles)

From the Culp's Hill Observation Tower, ride 0.25 miles downhill into Stevens' Knoll. The knoll connects Cemetery and Culp's Hills. It was named for Capt. Greenleaf T. Stevens, 5th Maine Artillery Battery. With the 33rd Massachusetts, Stevens' battery decimated the 57th North Carolina, who were attacking from the east, while also taking fire from the Louisiana Tigers, who were attacking from the north.

Views from the Culp's Hill Tower

The first photo shows the view looking northwest from the tower; the second is looking southwest.

Segment A2 (East Cemetery Hill)

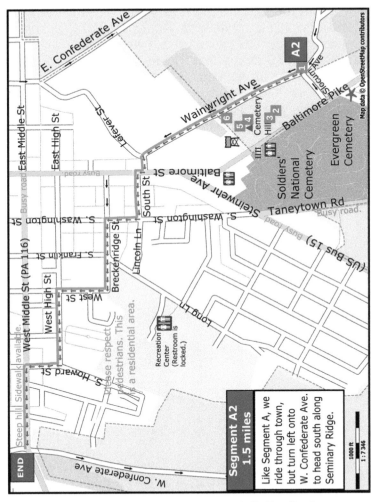

Map 2.4. Route 5 Segment A2 (1.5 miles)

Tip: To visit these monuments on foot, consider locking your group's bicycles together.

Segment A2 Cues (1.5 miles)

From Slocum Avenue at Wainwright Avenue to West Confederate Avenue, North End:	Seg	Total
0.0 STRAIGHT on Wainwright to tour East Cemetery Hill, to stop sign at Lefever	0.4	**2.7**
0.4 LEFT at Lefever to Baltimore. CROSS to sidewalk	0.5	**2.8**
0.5 RIGHT onto sidewalk, then LEFT on South for 1 block	0.6	**2.9**
0.6 RIGHT on S. Washington, then LEFT on Breckenridge to dead-end	0.9	**3.2**
0.9 RIGHT on West, then LEFT on W. High to dead-end on Howard	1.2	**3.5**
1.2 RIGHT on Howard, CROSS W. Middle to sidewalk, LEFT uphill to light	1.5	**3.8**

Table 2.1. Segment A2 Cues

Segment A2 Monument Highlights

The monuments in East Cemetery Hill mark the July 2–3 battlefield positions of many regiments in the 1st (Reynolds) and 11th (Howard) Corps, Army of the Potomac, under the command of Gen. George Meade. Located south of town, this high ground joined Culp's Hill to the main Union line along Cemetery Ridge and its terminus at Little Round Top, about one-mile south. Traditionally described as a fishhook formation, the "barb" was at Culp's Hill; the "bend" at East Cemetery Hill; and the "shank" was Cemetery Ridge.

1. 39.81990, -77.22617

2. 39.82098, -77.22875

3. 39.82132, -77.22889

4. 39.82165, -77.22888

5. 39.82195, -77.22888

6. 39.82264, -77.22811

1. 33rd Massachusetts Monument (1885)

With the 5th Maine Artillery Battery, the 33rd Massachusetts decimated the 57th North Carolina as they came at them from the east, and while the Louisiana Tigers fired upon them from the north.

2. 4th Ohio Monument (1887)

According to the monument inscription, the 4th Ohio was "hotly engaged in support of batteries on East Cemetery Hill until after 10 P.M." on July 2, 1863.

3. Winfield Hancock Equestrian Monument (1895–6)

Winfield Scott Hancock, nicknamed "Hancock the Superb," was a Pennsylvania native. He commanded the 2nd Corps of the Army of the Potomac, and was wounded southwest of here, during Pickett's Charge.

4. Oliver O. Howard Headquarters Monument

Maj. Gen. Howard established his headquarters on the high ground of East Cemetery Hill after ceding the town to the Army of Northern Virginia on July 1.

5. Oliver O. Howard Equestrian Monument (1932)

Oliver Otis Howard was from Maine. He commanded the 11th Corps of the Army of the Potomac, a group of mostly German immigrants.

6. 17th Connecticut Monument (1889)

On July 1, after retreating south from Barlow's Knoll, the 17th Connecticut fought here on East Cemetery Hill. Their commander, Lt. Col. Douglas Fowler, died from artillery fire while riding his white horse on the knoll.

Segment F2 (Seminary Ridge)

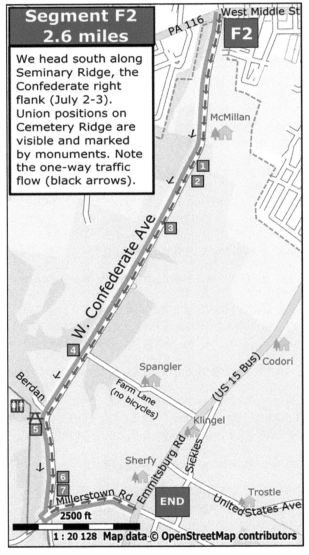

**Segment F2
2.6 miles**

We head south along Seminary Ridge, the Confederate right flank (July 2-3). Union positions on Cemetery Ridge are visible and marked by monuments. Note the one-way traffic flow (black arrows).

Map 2.5. Route 5 Segment F2 (2.6 miles)

Segment F2 Cues (2.6 miles)

North end of W. Confederate Avenue to The Peach Orchard at Emmitsburg Road:	Seg	Total
0.0 STRAIGHT (south) onto W. Confederate	1.1	**4.9**
1.1 From Virginia Monument, ride 1.1 miles	2.2	**6.0**
2.2 LEFT on Millerstown for 0.4 miles to stop at Emmitsburg Road	2.6	**6.4**

Table 2.2. Segment F2 Cues

Segment F2 Monument Highlights

The ride south on West Confederate Avenue follows Seminary Ridge on a relatively flat park road that overlooks farmland to the east. Segment F2 will end on the west side of The Peach Orchard and therefore not extend as far south as Warfield Ridge.

Most Confederate monuments at Gettysburg stand along this beautiful stretch of land, as this was Gen. Robert E. Lee's main battle line for his July 2–3, 1863 attacks on Union positions along Cemetery Ridge.

1. 39.81833, -77.24725

2. 39.81769, -77.24803

3. 39.81422, -77.25036

4. 39.81008, -77.25397

5. 39.80572, -77.25656

6. 39.80300, -77.25586

7. 39.80243, -77.25586

While riding Route 3b, you will visit six of the eleven Confederate state monuments that line Seminary Ridge. Each monument marks the state's starting position for attacks from this ridge on July 2–3, 1863.

1. North Carolina State Monument (1929)

The North Carolina State Monument faces east toward Union positions on Cemetery Ridge. From this location, Pettigrew's brigade joined Pickett's Charge.

2. Tennessee State Monument (1982)

This monument honors three regiments in Archer's brigade. It was the last Confederate state monument erected at Gettysburg.

3. Virginia State Monument (1917)

Virginia erected the first Confederate state monument at Gettysburg. It is the largest and most expensive Confederate monument in the park.

4. Florida State Monument (1963)

The three stars on the Florida State Monument represent the three regiments of Perry's brigade.

5. James Longstreet Equestrian Monument (1998)

Longstreet commanded Lee's 1st corps. This monument by sculptor Gary Casteel is the first anywhere dedicated to Lt. Gen. James Longstreet.

6. Louisiana State Monument (1971)

This monument depicts an iconic female figure hovering over a wounded Louisiana artilleryman.

7. Mississippi State Monument (1973)

This monument depicts a fallen color bearer and a Confederate soldier. It marks where Barksdale's brigade began its charge through The Peach Orchard.

Near the modern-day Virginia State Monument, you can see the fields of "Pickett's Charge":

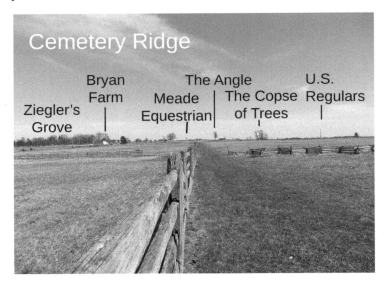

This view from the North Carolina State Monument shows the south end of the ridge at the Round Tops:

On July 2, Little Round Top became a major target for Confederate Lt. Gen. Longstreet's assault on the Union left. Here from the Longstreet Observation Tower, we see Little Round Top on the left (north) and Big Round on the right (south). Devil's Den is not visible, but it lies at the base of Little Round Top. You can see the Lewis Bushman farm in the mid-distance.

The next photo shows the 4th New York Independent ("Smith's") Battery monument in Devil's Den. Little Round Top is in the background.

Segment G2 (Little Round Top)

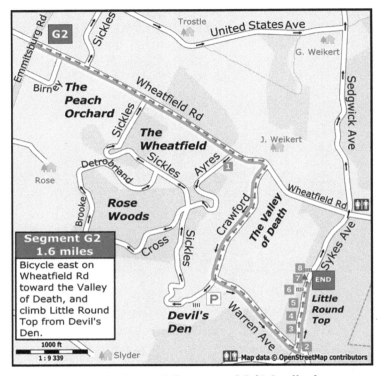

Map 2.6. Route 5 Segment G2 (1.6 miles)

As you cross Emmitsburg Road, note the slight elevation of the land relative to the fields farther east. This is where Union Maj. Gen. Dan Sickles posted his 3rd Corps guns on July 2 when he formed a salient from Cemetery Ridge that stretched thin the Union line in exchange for the high-ground advantage. The ride east on Wheatfield Road is a gentle descent through the Sherfy and Rose farms and into The Valley of Death below Little Round Top. The climb up Little Round Top is very steep (it is okay to walk your bike!).

Segment G2 Cues (1.6 miles)

The Peach Orchard at Emmitsburg Road to Little Round Top Parking Lot:		Seg	Total
0.0	CROSS Emmitsburg Road onto Wheatfield Road and ride 0.7 miles	0.7	**7.1**
0.7	RIGHT on Crawford for 0.3 miles to stop sign	1.0	**7.4**
1.0	LEFT on Warren for 0.4 miles to (confusing) intersection	1.4	**7.8**
1.4	LEFT uphill on Sykes for 0.2 miles to Little Round Top Parking Lot	1.6	**8.0**

Table 2.3. Segment G2 Cues

Tip: Lock your bicycle in the Little Round Top Parking Lot, then find monuments 2 through 8 on foot. Early morning is the least crowded time to visit.

Segment G2 Monument Highlights

1. 39.79700, -77.24017   **2.** 39.78947, -77.23617

Gettysburg National Military Park

3. 39.79095, -77.23710

4. 39.79095, -77.23711

5. 39.79127, -77.23713

6. 39.79144, -77.23703

7. 39.79217, -77.23672

8. 39.79253, -77.23667

Battle Days 2 & 3 Short Loop

1. 11th Pennsylvania Reserves (1890)

On the evening of July 2, Pennsylvanians drove the Confederates across The Valley of Death (your front right) and to The Wheatfield (your back right).

2. 83rd Pennsylvania Monument (1889)

This regiment's brigade commander, Strong Vincent, rallied soldiers to defend Little Round Top.

3. 20th Maine Monument (1889)

Joshua Chamberlain's regiment held the Union left flank against the 15th Alabama on Little Round Top.

4. Strong Vincent Wounded Monument (1878, 1978)

Beyond the national cemetery, this is Gettysburg's oldest marker for a mortally wounded soldier.

5. 44th and 12th New York Monument (1893)

This "castle" monument is the largest and most expensive regimental monument at Gettysburg.

6. 140th New York Monument (1889)

This monument stands near where its commander, Irish immigrant Patrick O'Rorke, died on July 2.

7. 91st Pennsylvania Monument (1889)

The Maltese cross on the top of this monument identifies Sykes' 5th corps.

8. Gouverneur K. Warren Statue (1888)

Army Chief Engineer Warren mobilized the 5th Corps to defend Little Round Top.

Segment H2

After visiting Little Round Top, ride north on Cemetery Ridge for 0.8 miles to tour the positions of the Union 5th (Gen. Sykes) and 6th (Gen. Sedgwick) Corps. This is the south end of the Union battle line.

Segment H2 Cues (0.8 miles)

Little Round Top Parking Lot to the Pennsylvania State Monument		Seg	Total
0.0	From Little Round Top Parking Lot, north (downhill) on Sykes to stop sign	0.3	**8.3**
0.3	STRAIGHT on Sedgwick (becomes Hancock) to PA State Monument	0.8	**8.8**

Table 2.4. Segment H2 Cues

Sedgwick Avenue

On this road named for Maj. Gen. John Sedgwick, monuments having a simple cross identify Sykes' 5th Corps; a Maltese cross, Sedgwick's 6th Corps. His equestrian and headquarters monuments are here:

Segment K (Cemetery Ridge)

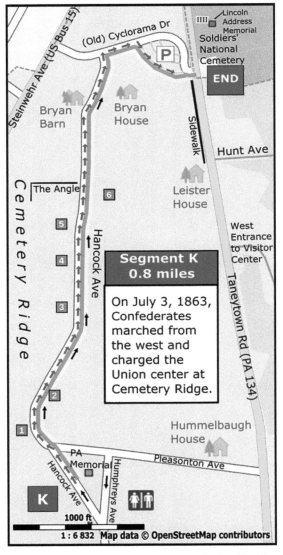

Map 2.7. Route 5 Segment K (0.8 miles)

Segment K Cues (0.8 miles)

Cemetery Ridge to Soldiers' National Cemetery Parking Lot:		Seg	Total
0.0	From the Pennsylvania State Monument, continue north for 0.6 miles to dead-end	0.6	**10.9**
0.6	RIGHT at dead-end and through parking lot to the Maryland State Monument, 0.8 miles	0.8	**11.1**

Table 2.5. Segment K Cues

1. 39.80876, -77.23705

2. 39.80942, -77.23650

1. Winfield S. Hancock Wounded Monument (1892)

During Pickett's Charge on July 3, Maj. Gen. Hancock was wounded in his right thigh near this location on Cemetery Ridge. He commanded the left wing of the Army of the Potomac under Gen. Meade.

2. Vermont State Monument (1889)

Vermont was the first state to erect a monument at Gettysburg. (In 2000, Delaware was the last).

3. 39.81124, -77.23575

4. 39.81246, -77.23570

5. 39.81319, -77.23587

6. 39.81397, -77.23492

3. U. S. Regulars Monument (1909)

Maj. Gen. George G. Meade's 95,000-man Army of the Potomac included over 7,000 federal ("Regular Army") soldiers, but most were volunteers from states.

4. High Water Mark, Copse of Trees (1892)

This monument's inscription honors the "patriotism and gallantry" of soldiers who repulsed Pickett's Charge on July 3. The trees are replanted versions of a copse on the battlefield ridge at the Union center.

The following photo was taken on the east side of Hancock Avenue (Cemetery Ridge), looking southwest over Emmitsburg Road toward the main Confederate battle line on Seminary Ridge. We are overlooking The Angle. South Mountain is in the distance.

The photo shows two very helpful landmarks for staying oriented on the Gettysburg battlefield. The first is the Codori Barn in the center of the photo. The barn is located on Emmitsburg Road, a road over which the Confederate army had to cross to attack the Union center line on July 3, 1863. Second, if you follow the road left (south), you can see the faint impression of the Longstreet Observation Tower at the end of Seminary Ridge. You may have noticed the tower while riding through The Peach Orchard in Segment J.

The Civil War era cannons that you see mark the positions of three artillery batteries: the Rhode Island Battery A (whose clover-topped monument is the rightmost monument in the photo), and also two artillery batteries from New York. You will want to walk your bike for at least the north half of Hancock Avenue, because this area is densely monumented—and there are many wayside exhibits to study.

Maps to Bike Gettysburg No. 3b   57

Segment L (Return)

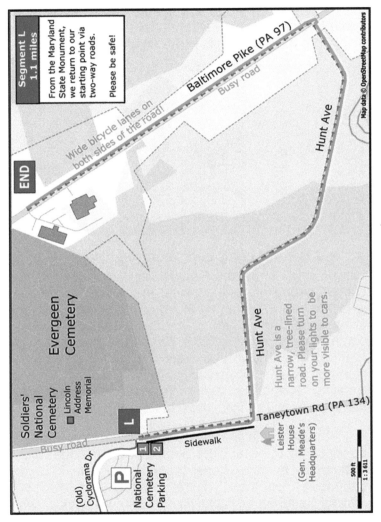

Segment L
1.1 miles

From the Maryland State Monument, we return to our starting point via two-way roads.

Please be safe!

Baltimore Pike (PA 97)

Busy road

Wide bicycle lanes on both sides of the road!

END

Hunt Ave

Map data © OpenStreetMap contributors

Soldiers' National Cemetery

Evergeen Cemetery

■ Lincoln Address Memorial

L

Hunt Ave

Hunt Ave is a narrow, tree-lined road. Please turn on your lights to be more visible to cars.

Taneytown Rd (PA 134)

Leister House (Gen. Meade's Headquarters)

1 2

Sidewalk

Busy road

(Old) Cyclorama Dr

P

National Cemetery Parking

500 ft

1 : 3 611

Map 2.8. Route 5 Segment L (1.1 miles)

Tip: There are two old bike racks in the cemetery.

Segment L Cues (1.1 miles)

From Soldiers' National Cemetery Parking Lot to Return to 945 Baltimore Pike:		Seg	Total
0.0	From Maryland State Monument, walk bike right (south) on sidewalk		**11.1**
	Follow Taneytown sidewalk to crosswalk at Hunt	0.1	**11.2**
0.1	CROSS Taneytown onto Hunt and continue to light at Baltimore Pike	0.7	**11.8**
0.7	LEFT on Baltimore Pike (wide shoulder for bicyclists) to starting point	1.1	**12.2**

Table 2.6. Segment L Cues

1. 39.81642, -77.23247

2. 39.81606, -77.23244

1. Maryland State Monument (1994)

The Maryland State Monument depicts a Union and Confederate soldier helping one another. Even though Maryland did not secede from the Union, men from Maryland fought in both armies at Gettysburg.

2. Delaware State Monument (2000)

The Delaware monument honors the state's Union and Confederate soldiers who fought at Gettysburg.

Pass the monument and follow the sidewalk along Taneytown Road to visit Gen. Meade's headquarters at the Lydia Leister property. The first photo shows the property as we face south toward Little Round Top (behind the Pennsylvania State Monument). Meade's army headquarters monument is in the second photo.

3.   What Next?

You did it! You cycled 10.7 miles along some of the most memorable portions of the Gettysburg battlefield. You learned about the Battle of Gettysburg while riding up Culp's Hill and Little Round Top. On the ride down Culp's Hill, you toured Cemetery Hill on your way to explore part of Seminary Ridge—before cutting east through The Peach Orchard and on to Cemetery Ridge.

I sincerely hope that you will want to return to Gettysburg and to explore more of its rich natural and physical landmarks, including more than 1,300 monuments and 400 refurbished Civil War cannons. In preparation for your next visit—or maybe to revive memories of your most recent ride—you will want to consult *Bicycling Gettysburg National Military Park: The Cyclist's Civil War Travel Guide*. This information-packed book describes a 23.8-mile tour of the entire park and includes numerous color photos of landmarks and historical monuments.

Guidebooks by Sue Thibodeau:

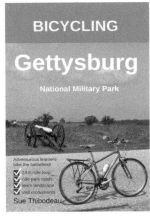

ISBN 9781732603806

286 pp, full-color
6"x9" perfect bound pbk

Published March 2019
by Civil War Cycling

www.civilwarcycling.com

Available for order at
your favorite book seller.

ISBN 9781732603813

208 pp, full-color
6"x9" perfect bound pbk

Published November
2020 by Civil War
Cycling

www.civilwarcycling.com

Available for order at
your favorite book seller.

Forthcoming Publications:

Bicycling Chickamauga Battlefield (2021)

Bicycling Shiloh National Military Park (2022)